BEYOND ALGORITHMS

THE ETHICAL BLUEPRINT OF AI LEADERSHIP

ALEJANDRO DABDOUB

ISBN 979-8-35092-765-8

DISCLAIMER

Alejandro Dabdoub is not a licensed financial advisor, broker, or trader. All commentaries expressed on the following pages are merely the author's personal opinions and therefore should not be considered or construed as instructions that will produce guaranteed results of any kind.

Furthermore, the reader acknowledges that, to the full extent permitted by law, the author:

1. does not accept any responsibility or liability for any results achieved by the reader,

2. whether or not said results arise from information provided in this book,

3. cannot be held liable for any business or investment loss or any direct, indirect, or

4. consequential loss resulting from any irregularity, inaccuracy, or use of the information contained herein, and

5. does not provide any warranties about the completeness, reliability, and accuracy of this aforementioned information.

Any action taken by the reader based upon information described on the following pages is strictly at the reader's own risk, and the author will not be held liable for any losses or damages resulting from the use of this publication.

ACKNOWLEDGMENT

First and foremost, I extend my deepest gratitude to my beautiful wife, Barbara. Her unwavering belief in me and her constant support have been the pillars upon which my dreams have been realized. To my children, Hanna, Patricio, and Lucia, your encouragement and faith in every endeavor of mine have been the driving forces behind my motivation. Your love and support mean the world to me. Lastly, a special thank you to Erik Scalavino. His invaluable insights, editing prowess, and creative ideas have played a pivotal role in shaping this book into the masterpiece it is today. To all of you, my heartfelt thanks.

CONTENTS

A STRANGE
NEW WORLD

As we approach the first quarter-century of this young millennium, technological innovations and advancements seem to be occurring at an unprecedented pace. The obvious benefits of these modern luxuries help make this an exciting time to be alive. Yet, there is a growing consensus, even among our world's most influential voices, that such rapid change is speeding beyond our collective control and jeopardizes our very existence as a species.

Never before in human history have ethical considerations associated with technology been more crucial. This is increasingly true in the realm of Artificial Intelligence (AI), which continues with terrifying velocity to infiltrate virtually every industry and facet of our lives.

While AI promises improved efficiencies, predictive insights, and even unparalleled breakthroughs, it also raises profound ethical questions. For example, how can we ensure this technology respects human dignity, promotes inclusivity, and benefits society as a whole? What principles should guide its development and integration?

In *Beyond Algorithms: An Ethical Blueprint for AI Leadership*, we explore these and other questions while embarking on an in-depth examination of the intersection between AI and ethics across the modern business landscape. Blending philosophy, real-world case studies, and expert perspectives, this publication provides a comprehensive map for leaders and developers to navigate thoughtfully and responsibly amid AI's meteoric rise.

Core themes of transparency, accountability, sustainability, and human-centric values form the framework of this blueprint. It challenges us to view AI not solely as a technological tool, but rather as an opportunity to reinforce our intrinsic humanity in the digital age. Furthermore, it serves as a call to consider timeless wisdom as we shape the progress of our cutting-edge innovations.

Whether we're developers crafting new algorithms, entrepreneurs integrating AI across operations, policymakers regulating its applications, or consumers who utilize technology, we all have a role to play in steering this technology towards ethical ends. By embracing the principles and practices outlined on the following pages, we can help realize AI's immense potential while ensuring that firm moral guideposts remain in place for posterity.

As the algorithmic era dawns, maintaining our human values amidst this dizzying change is admittedly no easy task, but perhaps our most critical one. AI can and should always exist to serve humanity, not overtake it. *Beyond Algorithms* provides an ethical blueprint to help us build a more just, inclusive, and uplifting future with AI as our ally, not our adversary.

CHAPTER 1

ARTIFICIAL INTELLIGENCE FROM YESTERDAY TO TODAY

"Imagination will often carry us to worlds that never were.
But without it, we go nowhere."

~ Carl Sagan

Before we begin our discussion and examination of Artificial Intelligence, perhaps it would be wise first to define the term and then put into context how we arrived at this moment. We'll trace its origins down through the ages to understand and appreciate how each technological breakthrough led to the next. Turns out, the AI systems we interact with today are part of an epic *human* story centuries in the making.

The term "Artificial Intelligence" dates back to the 1950s, when a group of Dartmouth College mathematicians coined the phrase to describe digital machines or computer-controlled robotic devices capable of human-level thought and function. Today, AI capabilities typically include data analysis and decision-making processes, speech and language translations, and visual perceptions, such as facial recognition. New applications and more powerful proficiencies continue to emerge with increased frequency.

Long before digital computers came to be, however, human minds envisioned thinking machines. In myths and legends across cultures, we find tales of artificial beings brought to life. The ancient Greeks spoke of Talos, a giant bronze automaton built to protect Europa. In Jewish folklore, the Golem of Prague carried out tasks on command. These and other stories reflected our timeless desire to recreate human capabilities within inorganic forms.

If necessity is the mother of invention, imagination may be its father. Every invention began as a dream in the inventor's mind. Visionaries and thought leaders throughout history envisioned a future where machines could emulate human skills like reason, language, and decision making. Their bold creativity emboldened others to turn fiction into reality.

In the 17th and 18th centuries, the Enlightenment and Industrial Revolution respectively erupted with mechanical ingenuity. Visionaries developed diverse automatic machines powered by springs, weights, and water, including Jacques de Vaucanson's digesting duck and Pierre Jaquet-Droz's autonomous android. These mechanical inventions could sing, write, and even play instruments with startling sophistication for their era. While limited in scope, they demonstrated the immense potential of machinic automation. This foundation of mechanical engineering established key design principles that would later inform computer AI.

By the 20th century, rapid advances in mathematics, logic, and electronics enabled creators to move past purely mechanical engineering towards far more versatile systems powered by electricity. The field of cybernetics emerged thanks to pioneers like Alan Turing, who conceptualized systems that could perform complex calculations and logical reasoning by manipulating symbols. The resulting successes led to further explorations of how information flows could mimic brain processes. The conceptual framework for AI as we know it today had been laid.

Then in 1937, the Atanasoff–Berry, the world's first electronic general-purpose computer, began to solve linear algebraic equations. The 1940s and '50s witnessed a huge leap towards general artificial intelligence when scientists developed the first programming languages to communicate with computers, which allowed precise instruction of computational tasks.

Another seminal moment came in summer 1956, when those aforementioned Dartmouth College scholars, including the renowned computer scientist John McCarthy, co-authored a pivotal document in which the term "Artificial Intelligence" first appeared. This galvanized both academia and industry to undertake extensive AI research projects. Scientists pursued natural language processing, computer vision, game theory, and countless subfields seeking to mimic facets of human intelligence – more bricks steadily being added to the foundation. Many predictions asserted that human-level AI was just around the corner, with some calling the era from the 1950s to the '70s the first golden age of AI.

During that time, researchers developed the first chatbot, called ELIZA, to converse with humans using pattern matching. Machine learning algorithms like the perceptron formed the basis for today's neural networks. While the seeds of modern AI began taking root, researchers still encountered challenges. Basic tasks like computer vision, speech recognition, and translation proved far more difficult than expected. Industry support began to wane by the end of the 1970s, now known as the first AI winter.

Just like the night is darkest before dawn, every winter invariably turns into spring. To overcome initial barriers to AI development, researchers focused on innovations in knowledge representation and expert systems, having recognized that AI requires vast knowledge bases and reasoning capabilities to make sense of the information it compiles. Knowledge bases such as Cyc aimed to codify millions of facts and rules about our world to provide AI technologies with greater context. Expert systems also simulated specialized skills by encoding domain knowledge from field experts. The resulting narrowed concentration produced deeper AI competencies.

Despite finding a measure of commercial success by the 1980s and '90s, these new knowledge-based approaches still hadn't addressed a glaring weakness in Artificial Intelligence: the inability of systems to learn on their own. AI research took on new life thereafter, with advances in processing power and neural network techniques driving this resurgence. Unlike earlier rule-based systems, neural nets mimicked biological brains, learning through examples without explicit programming. This enabled learning-based AI to master perceptual tasks involving complex, unstructured data including images, videos, and speech.

Long-standing challenges like facial recognition and real-time translation suddenly became more manageable – think computer vision, natural language, robotics, and more. Investments and enthusiasm in the sector surged as these rapid advancements demonstrated AI's immense practical potential. In the AI world, spring had indeed sprung.

Today, we live in a golden age of neural network AI, a veritable Cambrian explosion of AI applications built upon decades of methodical, foundational progress. Systems continue to achieve amazing new milestones, from AI beating grandmasters in Go to chatbots conversing with wit and nuance. Which is not to say that challenges don't remain. Current systems, for instance, lack true contextual understanding of their tasks. Consequently, any and all systems that are introduced from here on must be instilled with common sense reasoning, ethics, wisdom, and human values from the outset. This will help us realize AI's full potential while limiting its potential dangers.

AI's long story arc continues, and we retain the power to control its trajectory towards empowerment. Let's learn from the past as we chart humanity's shared future with AI. Elevating both technological and human progress will ensure that AI's powerful light benefits us all.

CHAPTER 2

HUMANS
IN AN
AI LANDSCAPE

"Everything you can imagine is real."

~ Pablo Picasso

Imagine for a moment that the future is not just some intangible, ephemeral moment in time, but in fact an enormous, luxurious mansion … and YOU hold the key to its front door. Each groove and curve on this key has been sculpted from dreams, aspirations, creative vision, and the ceaseless spirit of human potential. Each step to the front door of this mansion represents yet another in our collective journey of relentless progress as human beings. Such a key exists today. We call it Artificial Intelligence, or simply AI.

It's almost laughable to recall how computers were once gigantic machines that occupied entire rooms, when, nowadays, they can fit in the palms of our hands. Today's smart phones contain significantly more computing power than the guidance systems that NASA deployed to help land America's first astronauts on the moon in 1969.

Ever since, computers have evolved right alongside human beings, as both our limitless potentials have been and continue to be met and even exceeded in various aspects of life. AI's story, in effect, mirrors our own as well – one of breaking boundaries, of not just reaching for the stars, but also grasping them. Today, AI does so much more than play simple games; it predicts global trends, personalizes education, helps heal the sick, and even brings art to life. It's become more than technology; it's now a reflection of our deepest desires and our highest aspirations.

In many ways, we're now living in a present day that looks very much like the science fiction future we once envisioned. As we enter the atmosphere of this strange new world, let's never lose sight of this fact: AI is *our* creation, *our* masterpiece. Much like painters who imbue their soul into every brushstroke, we've infused AI with our universal human essence, our shared spirit. In the same way that every individual thought helps shape our unique realities, our collective intentions, values, and dreams will mold the future of AI.

To use another metaphor, our journey can be compared to an unfinished symphony, with AI playing an increasingly prominent role in the orchestra to help create a harmony of progress and potential. Yet, amidst all the algorithms and automation, the conductor of this orchestral masterpiece must remain the human spirit.

If every age in human history has had its defining medium, ours today is undoubtedly Artificial Intelligence. Having reshaped existing industries and given birth to new ones, AI has transformed our quotidian routines. Yet, this digital revolution would never have occurred without human ingenuity and ambition. We, the biological beings who dominate this planet, are the dreamers and creators who made this happen.

Down through the centuries, philosophers and visionaries of every stripe have authored their own versions of this universally accepted sentiment, that *"the only limits in our lives are those we impose on ourselves."* Yet, as we navigate the vast, relatively unexplored ocean that is AI, we must anchor ourselves with core values that reflect the limitless potential of our human spirit. Let's explore some of them:

Empathy – Every human interaction is a dance of emotions and energies. The true measure of AI will be in its ability to understand, respect, and consider the myriad emotions we experience. Algorithms that recognize patterns will be useless if those patterns fail to resonate with the heartbeat of humanity. True empathy taps into such energy, fostering genuine connections.

Integrity – In a world of infinite digital interactions, the cornerstone of trust remains our human bond. Whether a handshake promise or a complex algorithm, integrity is paramount in every relationship. AI should be a beacon of transparency and honesty, reflecting the trust we place in ourselves and in others.

Growth – Life at its best should be an endless journey of learning and evolution, powered by clear goals and unwavering focus. Similarly, our AI creations must inspire us, challenge our boundaries, and support personal and societal evolution as instruments that amplify our inherent drive for betterment, helping to keep us accountable as we strive for our highest potential.

Equity – True success and progress are inclusive outcomes. As we venture further into this digital age, no one should be left behind or on the margins. Our innovations must champion fairness and equality, commit to hearing every voice, respect every individual's dream, and provide everyone with a fair chance to realize those dreams and add their own unique value.

Stewardship – We are creators, yes, but also guardians. Every choice we make is like a stone dropped into a pond, sending ripples throughout the universe, impacting our environment, its finite resources, and the intricate web of life. As stewards of this digital realm, we must create technologies that respect, nurture, and protect the delicate balance of our world.

Faith and Spirituality – Regardless of our personal religious beliefs or non-beliefs, an undeniable spirit and energy reside at the core of every human being. While AI can compute and analyze powerfully, our role is to infuse that power with a sense of purpose that resonates with the larger universe, beyond any specific religion.

Personal Responsibility – With AI's growing ubiquity, we must recognize the intertwined relationship of its influence and our actions. We shape AI, but in tandem, our interactions with it shape our realities.

Visualization and Manifestation – In the better future we envision and long to establish, we must design AI systems that align with our intrinsic values.

Abundance Mindset – Rich in potential, AI should help us distribute its benefits equitably, thereby fostering an environment where all thrive.

Continuous Learning and Adaptability – Both humanity and AI must embrace a spirit of unceasing growth, refining themselves in alignment with evolving values.

Our ongoing odyssey with AI transcends mere technological achievement. It represents a profound opportunity for mortal beings to explore the timeless question, *"What is our place in the cosmos?"* In so doing, we are simultaneously unlocking seemingly bottomless reservoirs of innate potential. Novel AI trends occur almost daily, from neural architectures that emulate human cognition to systems that seamlessly integrate with our daily lives while redefining convenience and efficiency.

Thrilling though this whirlwind of innovation may be, the value of the human spirit must not be diminished as a result. For all its grandiose promise, AI needs to serve as a mirror that reflects our desires, dreams, and aspirations, shaped by our hands, guided by our intentions. As AI evolves, it must always draw its essence from our inherent self-worth.

Smarter cities, more-personalized healthcare, a fully interconnected global community. These are among AI's most dazzling potential advancements that can make our world a better place for ourselves and our offspring. Let us therefore embrace our role with the necessary sense of responsibility and reverence. We should never accept being mere bystanders in the AI revolution. We are its architects, its moral compass after all.

Certainly, we're exploring uncharted territory, the likes of which no other era in human history has witnessed. Let us illuminate the way forward with the light that never dims – the enlightened human mind. In the following chapters, we'll examine more closely how we might reasonably accomplish this.

CHAPTER 3

EMBRACING THE INEVITABLE – AI IN BUSINESS

"AI is a rare case where I think we need to be proactive in regulation [rather] than reactive."

~ Elon Musk

Change for the sake of change isn't always necessarily a good thing. As the age-old axiom advises us, *"If it ain't broke, don't fix it."* By the same token, it's also been famously observed by many throughout the centuries that the only constant in life *is* change. The degree to which that inevitable change impacts us depends in large part on our response to it. Either we can adapt to the new – regardless of how difficult letting go of the familiar can be – or remain committed to our preferred ways, the latter of which can leave us alone, isolated, or left behind.

Perhaps nothing in today's business world – the world in general, for that matter – represents change more than the advent of Artificial Intelligence. Pondering the universe of possibilities that AI offers in the realm of global commerce can be like gazing up at the limitless expanse of the night sky, its countless stars twinkling like so many of our most precious dreams.

What do we envision for the future of businesses: Companies seamlessly predicting market trends? A better understanding of intricate consumer behaviors? More efficiently managed resources? Yes, to all of these and probably more. Businesses will no longer operate on mere intuition, but be empowered by more precise data-driven insights, offering products and services tailored so personally to individual needs that it would seem almost magical.

AI promises such automation and efficiency. However, a company's ultimate success will hinge on its ability to integrate core values into its AI technologies. Organizations can utilize the most advanced AI systems, but without values like we discussed in Chapter 2 – empathy, integrity, stewardship, et cetera – such technologies may lack direction, purpose, and soul.

Artificial Intelligence is already widespread and quickly becoming omnipresent in business. Supply chains will soon be more capable of predicting and adapting instantly to global shifts, keeping businesses prepared for any potential disruptions. Customer service chatbots will not only resolve issues more frequently, but also with such understanding and empathy that consumers might forget they're not interacting with a real person. Production processes will be optimized to utmost precision so as to waste neither time nor resources.

Beyond these tangible benefits, AI could also help businesses forge deeper personal connections and genuine relationships with consumers by better understanding their desires, fears, and dreams. With the implied trust that underpins these strengthened bonds comes an immense responsibility for businesses and their leaders. The power they wield as a result of AI must be applied judiciously and equitably so that any biases, unintended or otherwise, are not introduced. Stewardship will become even more pivotal as companies certify that their AI solutions are sustainable and not depleting resources or causing environmental harm.

Let's look now at a powerhouse company that provides us with one such early example.

CASE STUDY: STARBUCKS BREWS PERSONALIZED EXPERIENCES WITH AI

Coffee lovers might already know the joy of strolling into their favorite neighborhood café, where everybody knows everybody else, and, without uttering a word, the barista begins preparing their favorite drink, just the way they like it. Starbucks harnessed the power of AI to magnify this intimate, small-town experience on a global scale.

A world-renowned brand synonymous with innovation, Starbucks didn't just embrace AI, they made it an intrinsic part of their business model as well. Their mobile app, used by millions worldwide, is designed not just a payment or ordering system. Fundamentally, it's an AI-driven engine that learns from every purchase, every preference, and every click. By analyzing this data, the Starbucks app offers personalized drink recommendations and rewards tailored to individual preferences. It even predicts busiest store times to help staff with inventory and shift planning.

Remarkably, Starbucks has managed to integrate AI without sacrificing its human touch or core values. The popular company's brand has always been, as Starbucks' marketing puts it, about *"inspiring and nurturing the human spirit – one person, one cup, and one neighborhood at a time."* AI complements this mission by making sure every customer feels seen, valued, and understood, even in the digital realm. It's a beautiful amalgamation of technology meeting tradition, of tomorrow shaking hands with today, if you will, and paying homage to yesterday.

Starbucks also seems to understand the importance of stewardship. They've been transparent about their use of data, emphasizing customer privacy and ensuring their digital endeavors align with their foundational principles of trust and community.

Like Starbucks, let's think big, even bigger than before. AI won't just be a part of our businesses; it will become an integral facet of our companies' identities, reflecting our values, aspirations, and ethos. It's not hyperbole to assert that businesses who'll thrive are those that view AI as a reliable partner more than a simple tool.

It's a wondrous, star-filled universe of infinite potential. But as businesses adopt a mindset of embracing this AI-infused future, they must never abandon their core values and always remain true to their mission of providing value, meaning, and enrichment to the lives of the people they serve. As they say, some things never change.

CHAPTER 4

AI – AN ETHICAL MIRROR

"We are not being true to the inventor of the first computer
until we admit that the real value of a computer isn't in
its speed or its size, but in its ethics."
~ Tom Watson, IBM founder

L ike a seed taking root in fertile ground, every invention, every idea, every technological leap forward begins as a mere thought in a person's mind. It then germinates and grows, but can only reach its full potential if nurtured by our values and intentions. Just as some visionaries and noetic scientists believe that our thoughts have the ability to become tangible objects and events, we, as creators of Artificial Intelligence, must always remember these innovations that we birth are profound reflections of our intentions, beliefs, and biases.

History provides numerous examples of moments when humanity developed a groundbreaking technology that raised complex ethical and existential questions. When the printing press first spread across Europe in the 15th century, this revolutionary mechanical device became both a modern convenience and a powerful symbol of the democratization and proliferation of knowledge. For the first time ever, books, news, and ideas could be mass-produced, distributed, and disseminated to wider populaces, thus challenging the information monopoly previously enjoyed only by elite and religious classes. At the same time, this led people to ask who would control the newfound power of mass communication, and whether limits should be placed on what could or could not be printed.

This recurring pattern continued in the 20th century with the advent of radio and television, media that radically transformed how people shared and consumed information. Audio and video content could be broadcast to millions simultaneously, regardless of geographical distances. But who would be tasked with overseeing its scope, reach, and regulation? Once again, an intoxicating technology had outpaced existing ethical governance, forcing society to reconcile long-held values with emerging capabilities.

We witnessed the theme yet again at the turn of the 21st century as the explosive growth of the internet shattered geographical barriers even further. The worldwide web provided a global gathering point for communication, commerce, and community, while also introducing thorny new ethical challenges related to online privacy, data ethics, misinformation, and cybercrime. Creators and users alike struggled – and continue to struggle – to define and agree on ethical norms for this digital frontier.

Today, with AI rapidly becoming mainstream, we've arrived at yet another historical inflection point. From facial recognition to predictive algorithms, AI promises to reshape society. But developers, companies, and governments are grappling with the immense ethical implications of deploying machines that are programmed to learn and think. With history as our guide, we cannot advance AI without questioning how it aligns with our deepest human values.

If every algorithm and piece of code reflects its creator, these reflections become magnified exponentially in the realm of AI. Should a coder's or a company's biases seep into its AI system, even unintentionally, those partialities can spread rapidly and globally, potentially affecting millions in a negative or harmful way.

For example, studies of facial recognition technologies have revealed some potentially troubling findings. In 2018, a study conducted by the Massachusetts Institute of Technology (MIT) found that facial recognition software had error rates of up to 35 percent when identifying darker-skinned women, compared to error rates of less than 1 percent for lighter-skinned men. This apparent racial and gender imbalance in the software's algorithms seemed to reflect human prejudices on a massive scale.

Researchers such as Dr. Timnit Gebru, formerly the co-leader of Google's Ethical Artificial Intelligence Team, have dedicated their careers to studying unintended biases in AI systems. Dr. Gebru's groundbreaking work has shown that without careful examination, AI models can amplify human biases around race, gender, and ethnicity in harmful ways.

This technological concern actually dredges up much deeper ethical issues. Certainly, debugging computer codes is crucial, but truly addressing algorithmic biases may require our grappling with complex historical and cultural dynamics. AI offers us an opportunity to confront long-standing prejudices, but only if we summon the courage to inspect very carefully the mirror it holds up.

Of course, ethics can vary greatly by any number of demographic measurements: culture, geography, religion, and individual perspectives, to name a few. For instance, China's perspective on facial recognition technology in public spaces differs significantly from attitudes in Europe. Google's internal AI ethics are likely distinct from those of an emerging startup. A programmer based in, say, Nigeria may view data privacy differently than a coder in Chile.

While AI systems may not recognize borders, their ethical concerns may not be universally accepted when deployed globally, unless its codes and frameworks were adjusted to conform to localized considerations. Our shared core human values of empathy, integrity, growth, equity, stewardship, faith, and spirituality can therefore act as a moral compass. Yet, it remains the responsibility of each nation, community, and individual to chart AI's ethical course in conjunction with respective cultural nuances. We must engage in open, honest, ongoing dialogue, embracing both common ground and disagreement, to guide AI thoughtfully. Few easy answers exist, but we need to commit to an earnest ethical exploration.

At its most basic, AI consists of human-crafted algorithms and data models whose potential to transform society, as we've established on previous pages, is enormous. Within health care, AI promises earlier disease detection, personalized medicine, and life-saving clinical insights. In education, it can enable customized instruction across topics and grade levels. And in business, AI is already boosting efficiency, productivity, and innovation. The benefits encompass nearly every industry and professional field, but they come with a critical condition: ethics.

Our rapid technological advancements must reflect our core human values. Otherwise, we risk compromising basic principles of privacy, equity, safety, and human rights. For example, deploying facial recognition on a city-wide level may improve overall security levels, but could also lead to over-surveillance and infringement of civil liberties on particular communities or populations. Powerful natural language algorithms may generate helpful content, but could also be hijacked to spread deliberate misinformation. As AI's capabilities grow, we cannot simply ask, "Can we build this?" but also, "Should we?" before unleashing them at scale.

This requires human oversight, combating unfair bias, and protecting privacy. Ethics must be foundational from the very first lines of AI code, not an afterthought. We must therefore all embrace active roles as stewards of ethical AI. Here are some carefully considered suggestions for how to proceed:

AI Developers

- Take responsibility for examining your own internal biases.
- Question any assumptions baked into codes.
- Proactively debug unfairness in algorithms.
- Foster a culture of transparency and accountability within teams and organizations.

Business Leaders

- Audit your AI systems for potential harms, such as discriminatory outcomes or loss of human autonomy.
- Establish oversight procedures, impact assessments, and grievance redressal processes.
- Enact mechanisms to remedy issues promptly.
- Treat AI ethics as fundamental to strategy, not peripheral.

Policymakers

- Develop appropriate regulations to safeguard citizens' rights while promoting AI innovation.

- Bring diverse stakeholders together to find balanced policy solutions.

- Invest in educational initiatives that teach both AI technical skills and ethics.

Everyday Citizens and Users

- Stay informed on AI developments.

- Think critically about their risks, not just their benefits.

- Make conscientious choices about AI interactions.

Together, our voices and values must guide societal adoption of AI. Codes that power today's AI may seem impossibly complex to most of us, but the human ethics behind them needn't be. By rooting ourselves in justice, responsibility, and dignity, we become active shepherds of AI and its advancement. Only then can humanity harness AI's immense power for good and AI truly begin to enhance, rather than undermine, human dignity and potential.

CHAPTER 5

THE RESPONSIBILITY OF LEADERSHIP

"Leadership is not about titles, positions, or flowcharts.
It is about one life influencing another."
~ John C. Maxwell

Much like people become wayward souls without a moral compass to guide them, AI without human leadership will never fulfill its limitless potential for doing good. With us to steward it and infuse the technology with meaning and purpose, there's no telling what wonderful things AI can achieve. As I and others are fond of saying, *"The only limits in life are those we impose on ourselves."*

Have you ever heard a song for the first time and it just spoke to you? Despite its newness, it somehow felt instantly familiar to your heart. Today's leaders must be attuned to the fact that certain timeless melodies resonate with the human spirit. Not musical melodies, mind you, but the values that live within each of us – even if in some cases they might be dormant.

As this relates to Artificial Intelligence, the speed, precision, and scale that it promises are tantalizing. Yet as beautiful as this may sound, our leaders must make it even more harmonious by imbuing AI with the kind of meaningful values that speak to each human heart.

In every area of business, from factory floors to customer interfaces and beyond, technology offers alluring potential: cost savings, efficiency, reach, et cetera. However, without the personal touch, the empathy, and the compassion behind choices that builds strong human connections, the tune will fall flat. Every organization must therefore nurture both technological capability and human community.

Certainly, it can be a delicate balance for today's leaders to strike. Lean too far towards cold efficiency and you risk becoming mechanical and faceless. But if the pendulum swings too far towards the analog past, organizations may not keep pace with changes. Finding that equilibrium between innovating with technology while amplifying, not sacrificing, what makes us profoundly human is therefore paramount.

For AI, this begins with data, the raw material. Human wisdom then serves as the refining force that conveys meaning to that data. Information alone can overwhelm and obscure. Which is why we need discerning, ethical minds that operate on human values to transmute data into enriching strategies that serve all people and guide us towards empowerment and justice.

Every AI system begins as a blank canvas, absorbing the brushstrokes of its creators. Our best intentions and core values should be those first brushstrokes. Just as children reflect their upbringing, we must cultivate AI with wisdom and care so that whatever we program into it mirrors our most honorable characteristics.

For example, customer service chatbots designed with emotional intelligence can detect subtle human cues and respond with compassion. This fuses technological capability with human empathy into a tool that enhances communication. We must always craft AI not for mere efficiency but with the aim of deepening our human connections. In today's ever-evolving, fast-paced business landscape, technology provides the rhythm, but our values, our ethics, and our principles create the inspiring, heartfelt melody that truly resonates with humanity.

Before implementing any Artificial Intelligence, an organization must bear this in mind and be unequivocally clear regarding its core values and how they translate into this new technological age. With values as their anchor, organizations can adopt AI in ways that thoughtfully serve community – a greater purpose than mere profits.

Furthermore, by rooting themselves in continuous learning and adaptation, organizations and their leaders can more than withstand rapid change, but also guide that change toward a more justice future. A culture that honors collective wisdom, through diverse feedback and perspectives, will flourish harmoniously with equal parts ethics and innovation.

The choices we leaders make today will echo across decades, shaping our peers and cementing our legacies. When confronting the complexities of AI, leaders must recognize their decisions will become the bedrock upon which industry is built for generations to come. Leaders who champion ethics, diversity, and human dignity in AI will see those choices permeate boardrooms for years to come. Our insistence upon transparency and accountability will become pillars of best practices. As such, we are pioneers laying the ethical foundations for the AI future.

Of course, the opposite also holds true. Leaders who ignore AI's downsides and potential pitfalls risk enabling and being held responsible for long-term harms. Their lack of wisdom and foresight will cast dark shadows, rather than soothing light, across the AI frontier. Thus, every leader today has the potential to be an author who helps write the opening chapters that will be examined by generations to come. The tone we set, the vision we share, and the guardrails we implement will impact millions – even billions – who've not yet been born.

True leadership requires a more altruistic perspective that looks beyond quarterly returns. As we journey deeper into the AI age, leadership can become artistry. Leaders are the conductors, orchestrating a symphony where technology and humanity harmonize beautifully. Our legacy will not just be the AI tools we build, but, more importantly, the values we instill in them. We have the power to be maestros of our shared future. Let us compose wisely and fill it with a hope that resonates with everyone.

CHAPTER 6

SURVIVING THE ETHICAL MINEFIELD

"AI is a tool. The choice about how it gets deployed is ours."

~ Oren Etzioni

A t this point in our exploration, you've probably caught on to the fact that I love metaphors and analogies. If you'll indulge me once again, I'd like to employ yet another.

An artist uses paint and a brush – perhaps a pallet knife and other tools as well – to create something beautiful and original. The artist's vision and skill are what bring the work of art to life, however. Likewise, human beings are the artists who created Artificial Intelligence, a technology that can be both the work of art itself and the brush we choose to augment our creativity, wisdom, and potential.

Any tool, from a paint brush to a hammer to an algorithm, can drive progress or deliver pain, depending on the intentions of the hand that wields it. As its artists, we should nurture our creation from the beginning with empathy, ethics, and emotional intelligence, so that it always serves as our ally and never as an adversary.

Throughout this book, we've cited numerous examples of how AI can revolutionize medicine, sustainability, education, and more by improving our desired outcomes in terms of accuracy, speed, and scale. Yet, just like any minefield has a safe route through it, hidden dangers still lurk not far below the surface. AI's increasingly symbiotic relationship with human beings offers infinite potential for the common good, but, if left in the wrong hands, also comes with inherent risks of misuse in areas such as surveillance, deception, and control.

Furthermore, AI's obvious conveniences and alluring promise to augment our lives can lead some of us to neglect or even forget our own inarguable self-worth. We can never allow ourselves to diminish our inherent value as unique, individual human beings. Our dreams, our creativity, and our capacity to love, to cite a few examples, separate us distinctly from the machines we develop, however wonderful they might be.

We may joke that we don't know where we'd be today with our technologies – our cell phones, laptops, tablets, and other indispensable devices. But we can never allow ourselves to think that we humans are irreplaceable. AI and other modern conveniences are just tools that should serve humanity, not supplant it in any way. In our hands, AI can be channeled for justice, empowerment, and universal human dignity.

Throughout human history, we've been a species with an inherent spirit of adventure. Brave pioneers, intrepid explorers, eager to venture into uncharted territory to satisfy – at least momentarily – our insatiable curiosity.

Once more, we find ourselves on the verge of a new frontier to investigate, a digital landscape increasingly dominated by Artificial Intelligence. As we set forth into it, we must proceed with caution and care, as though it were a minefield, trusting our moral compass to guide us safely into and through the unknown.

Our AI journey will undoubtedly present further challenges, some as yet unforeseen, that could severely test our principles. But such challenges also present opportunities for our moral growth. Organizations such as the United-Kingdom-based Institute for Ethical AI & Machine Learning are helping in this regard by establishing vital ethical guidelines.

Meanwhile, each of us possesses the most reliable of tools to navigate this potentially treacherous minefield – a conscience, that honest inner voice to which we can always turn and listen when the way forward becomes confusing.

CHAPTER 7

THE AI-CUSTOMER RELATIONSHIP

"Artificial Intelligence would be the ultimate version of Google,
the ultimate search engine that would … understand exactly
what you wanted and give you the right thing ...
That is basically what we work on."

~ Larry Page

Let's face it – change is almost always difficult. Even change for the better takes some getting used to, because as exciting as the change may be, we humans are innately fearful of the unknown. As it's been said, *"The devil you know is better than the devil you don't."*

Change is necessary, however, as well as inevitable. Transformational change – whether personal, societal, technological, or otherwise – often sparks unease. Throughout history, humans have met new innovations with a combination of wonder and wariness. We see this happening once again as the new AI era dawns. And once more, we can learn from our collective past to help us adapt to this new future.

From the steam engine to electricity to the internet, whenever new technologies emerged in our lives and societies, we met them with immediate apprehension, our naturally human instinct in the face of the unfamiliar. Yet, our initial skepticism yielded to eventual reliance on those past innovations. Likewise with AI, we can expect to become comfortable with it sooner or later. But this will require laying a foundation of transparency, education, and trust from the very start.

Earlier in this book, we touched on the printing press example. Inventor Johannes Gutenberg's revolutionary machine had more than its fair share of skeptics in 15th century Europe, but gradually, the hysteria subsided as the overwhelming majority of people recognized the printing press' benefits far outweighed any potential risks. Proponents of the printing press required much patience while the invention took decades to win over the general populace.

With time, transparency, and education around its capabilities, apprehension toward the printing press gave way to acceptance. The same cycle has repeated itself with subsequent technological leaps. And now, with AI rapidly advancing, we have the opportunity to accelerate this transition, creating broader understanding and trust from the outset. Trust, of course, is essential for any relationship to thrive, especially the one we're cultivating between ourselves and these thinking machines we're developing.

In light of this fact, computer giant Microsoft has proposed six principles for responsible AI development which can help provide valuable guidance:

MICROSOFT'S PRINCIPLES FOR RESPONSIBLE AI DEVELOPMENT

- Fairness

- Reliability and Safety

- Privacy and Security

- Inclusiveness

- Transparency

- Accountability

It's reassuring to note that Microsoft agrees that transparency must play a crucial role when building trust. Because, for the average person today, AI remains too complex to comprehend. Learning how technologies function – being able to look under the hood, if you will – helps ease our natural fear of the unknown and make it more familiar. We must therefore explain AI's inner-workings using clear communications, removing all technical jargon and esoteric language, to tout its capabilities in plain, layman's terms that anyone can understand.

Demystifying AI will be imperative to building trust and acceptance. For example, when people understand how self-driving cars analyze visual data, or how smart speakers comprehend our commands, consumers become active participants rather than passive users, while AI goes from opaque technology to indispensable tool.

Even after trust has been established, AI must remain the assistant to the master human.

Designs should always focus on amplifying human potential, not overshadowing or usurping it, and providing a helping hand where we fall short. In conjunction with transparency, we must actively and continually educate people about AI's workings, potentials, and boundaries. Knowledge is power, after all, and ongoing education is yet another key to nurturing a healthy AI relationship with consumers.

Consider chatbots like Alexa, Clara, or Siri. To set a precedent of respectful engagement, companies that create and use such technologies should explain how they work, in the simplest terms – that they process language, identify patterns, but lack human general intelligence.

Furthermore, our interaction with AI must always be a two-way street. Companies should provide not only ongoing opportunities for user feedback, but also visible, tangible responses to customers' questions and concerns. This helps refine the AI to be more helpful and signals to users that their perspectives are valued. Consumers are thereby encouraged to become more invested participants in shaping AI. Rather than an imperious, top-down push, ethical AI integration should be driven by symbiotic collaboration with everyday consumers, steering its evolution towards justice and uplifting both sides.

As we've stated continuously throughout this book, AI systems cannot be evaluated on their efficiency alone. Their success hinges equally on being embedded with moral wisdom and aligned with human ethics and dignity. AI design processes should begin first with an examination of the system through a philosophic lens, then a technological one.

For example, unchecked machine learning algorithms risk amplifying our human prejudices, as we've discussed in previous chapters. Inspecting for biases during development, rather than after the fact, allows creators to remedy potential issues proactively. Ethics cannot be an afterthought, but woven throughout the AI process.

As AI designs become more participatory, as education dissolves the aura of mystery surrounding them, and as trust strengthens through transparency, our partnership with AI will blossom, leading to ever more human-centric intelligent systems capable of dignifying life.

CHAPTER 8

INCLUSIVE AI

"We need … a better system of checks and balances to test AI for bias and fairness, and to help businesses determine whether certain use cases are even appropriate for this technology at the moment."

~ Timnit Gebru

I n an ideal world, every tool and innovation would be designed not for the privileged few but for all of humanity in its gorgeous mosaic of diversity. AI can be such an inclusive technology that enriches and uplifts every life. At their best, inclusive AI systems would serve not just the majority but the entirety of our human family. They would embrace human-kind's intricate spectrum of languages, cultures, abilities, and experiences.

Across the developing world, so-called "smallholder farmers" depend on themselves and their limited resources alone to grow crops and food products. Unlike more sophisticated and technologically elaborate urban populations, these rural farmers face numerous disproportionate challenges from climate change, lack of infrastructure, and other contributing factors. Inclusive AI systems could serve as a great equalizer.

Microsoft's FarmBeats initiative shows us how this might be done. Using Artificial Intelligence and sensors to provide crucial agricultural insights on crop timing, soil conditions, and other relevant criteria, FarmBeats allows smallholder farmers worldwide to access the most modern technologies anywhere in the world. This democratization of AI expands empowerment even to society's most marginalized communities, thereby helping to spread knowledge and dignity to improve people's lives.

Like the FarmBeats example, AI applications in healthcare, education, and accessibility – if properly designed and implemented – can help underprivileged individuals and groups worldwide realize their full potential while leading dignified, purposeful lives. Every algorithm and line of code contained therein should resonate with love, respect, and service for others, or else our AI systems risks expanding our existing divides.

Inclusivity in AI doesn't simply mean recognizing diverse faces or languages. It must also be thoughtfully crafted to understand, cherish, and cater to the unique strengths and needs of every individual and community. AI should help amplify marginalized voices rather than silence or restrict them, to remove barriers rather than erect them, to encourage the values of care, compassion, and equity fundamental to human dignity. As such, AI can become a force for promoting justice and empowerment for all, regardless of demographic.

In today's increasingly fractured world, AI-driven advancements hold enormous potential to unify us or, if applied negligently, to drive us further apart. So, let us cling to that vision of an ideal world, assisted by inclusive AI that is designed, refined, and guided by diverse voices, irrespective of language, gender, race, or creed.

The responsibility rests with us, the institutions, corporations, and governments plotting and steering AI's trajectory. As such, we must shape AI as an instrument to empower, not exploit. Our profound task is no less than to develop and guide Artificial Intelligence for the benefit of all humankind, today and for generations to come.

CHAPTER 9

PROGRESS ANCHORED IN PURPOSE

"If Artificial Intelligence fouls up society,
then how intelligent was it, really?"
~ Neil deGrasse Tyson

Each new day is a blessing filled with opportunity for achievement, advancement, and change for the better. Artificial Intelligence promises all this, as we've detailed throughout the previous pages. In our excitement over progress, however, we cannot forget purpose – our overarching commitment to human rights, justice, and morality, embracing new tools while staying anchored to timeless human virtues.

Today's leaders face a defining choice. Will we steer this powerful force with a moral compass aligned to elevating humanity? Or will we blindly adopt AI in the name of advancement, compromising ethics in the process? AI is already reshaping our lives and will continue to do so. But its ultimate, lasting impact hinges entirely on the values instilled within it.

Our collective duty, then, is to infuse this new power with our human empathy, compassion, and spirit of service towards others. If centered on respect for human dignity, individuality, and diverse cultures, AI can be crafted to enrich society rather than control it.

This requires continuous, lifelong learning and making space for personal and collective growth amidst ever-increasing pressures. Individuals and organizations must zealously commit to regular education, adapting to new tools while also deepening and refining human proficiencies like creativity, critical thinking, communication, and ethical reasoning. These time-honored skills enable us to move forward more confidently and with moral clarity.

Consider the example of Unilever. In recent years, the multinational consumer goods company adopted AI technology for parts of its hiring process, using algorithmic games and video interviews to assess human attributes such as problem-solving ability, diction, and body language. This resulted in enhanced efficiency, reduced hiring time, and notably, increased workforce diversity.

However, Unilever's experience also raises serious ethical questions. For instance, is it appropriate to evaluate candidates based on minute facial expressions and micro-gestures? Could biases seep into algorithms determining aptitude? Increasingly, the rapid integration of AI leads to certain immediate benefits, but also unforeseen risks that require ongoing and transparent examination.

To prevent any such negative or counterproductive results, organizations must build robust mechanisms allowing them to inspect AI implementations, identify emerging issues, and course-correct responsively. Technology will continue advancing, but wisdom demands ongoing introspection so that progress never compromises human dignity and justice.

Even as AI and automation radically reshape how we operate in the workplace, our underlying need for collective purpose and human connection remains. By consciously building work environments where diverse people unite through shared vision, ethics, and camaraderie, we counteract emerging trends toward isolation and fragmentation, reaffirming that we are social beings who are better together than alone.

None of us thrives in isolation, either as individuals, groups, or organizations. Real fulfillment stems not just from personal success, but from uplifting each other. Even amidst rapid technological change, we must nurture community, empathy, and collaboration. When united by ethical purpose, we can achieve far more together than individually. AI should serve as a bridge connecting diverse voices and ideas, bonding humanity in a spirit of service.

Absent the stable ground that our shared wisdom and morality provide, AI risks causing further inequity and division in our global society. Capitalizing on technology while sacrificing ethics only guarantees fleeting progress followed by profound strife. Our purpose is therefore no less than to unlock human potential and nourish the soul, with AI as our trusted tool that transcends mere code and hardware.

Our modern innovations and devices will one day be relics of history, just as each one of us will return to the ashes and dust from which we were formed. However, the values we embed within our technological creations will continue inspiring and serving the generations who will follow after us.

CHAPTER 10

OUR CALL TO ACTION – DIGNIFYING LIFE WITH AI

"Computers will overtake humans with AI at some point. When that happens, we need to ensure AI's goals align with ours."

~ Stephen Hawking

I like to think of these wise words by Stephen Hawking, one of the great geniuses of our time, not as a prophecy of ruin, but a clarion call to shape AI with ethics and vision. Not as a vision of man versus machine, but of man collaborating with machine to achieve what neither could alone. Just as a telescope expands our visual capabilities and a calculator empowers mathematical reasoning, AI designed as a tool that augments human skills, when combined with human strengths like intuition, empathy, and ethics, can enhance our problem-solving, creativity, and decision-making.

Where we stand with Artificial Intelligence today is but a glimpse of what lies ahead. In decades and centuries to come, AI will most certainly be far more integrated across our world, more intuitive, and more indispensable to future human beings – a promising yet somewhat unnerving prospect. By understanding our responsibilities with respect to AI today, generations to come will benefit and give thanks for our foresight.

For businesses and their leaders, this starts with remembering and reinforcing the fact that every organization's true strength lies in its people. No system, no matter how technologically brilliant, can match the spirit, imagination, and purpose behind human minds that are united by a common vision. Our people should always power our progress. Organizations should always nourish a culture where people feel respected, empowered, and responsible. Employees should understand their role in applying any new technologies for the benefit of all people, starting within their own communities.

Let's further commit to fostering dialogue that encourages each person to discern his or her own unique gifts and purpose, while determining how they can uplift others. This sense of meaning enables people to approach innovations like AI as tools for service rather than merely for profit. I've found that employees who are treated with respect tend to pass on that respect through their work. Consequently, if people feel connected to ethical aspirations bigger than themselves, they'll undoubtedly help steer their organizations towards conscientious AI adoption.

As business leaders, let's reaffirm our shared mission to build enlightened, purpose-driven cultures within our organizations. Workplaces, for example, that cultivate relationships based on trust, care, and mutual human dignity; that promote diversity and inclusion, where all voices and backgrounds are valued; that provide opportunities for ongoing education and growth; that develop mechanisms for transparency in AI systems and accountable leadership; that maintain openness to input and feedback from all levels.

When implementing Artificial Intelligence into our workplaces, let's also ensure that they enhance people's talents, not supersede them. For instance, an AI writing assistant could empower authors with research and editing support rather than replace them.

Embedding ethical AI requires instilling human values throughout organizational culture. Employees surrounded by accountability, justice, and transparency will intuitively help design AI systems which reflect these principles. Ethics naturally flow from how people are treated every day. Organizations that encourage and uplift human dignity will discover AI's capabilities elevating their impact exponentially.

Leadership of this kind requires courage to look beyond our balance sheets and champion timeless virtues. Yet, if organizations adopt AI to unlock deeper human potential, both employee and customer experiences will flourish. AI offers great power, but such power without moral oversight will invariably corrupt. So, let's agree to lead by listening to diverse voices, planting seeds of human values within our teams, and wielding AI as a tool for invigorating human potential across all communities.

May our legacy be one where technologies like AI were crafted first and foremost to spread justice, empowerment, and joy through the elevation of our shared humanity. We owe this to ourselves, our ancestors, and our posterity.

Today, some 1.3 billion Catholics look to Pope Francis, the Church's affable and indefatigable leader, for moral guidance. Reflecting on the future of AI and its place in modern society, the Holy Father has emphasized the importance of ensuring that AI and technology at large always remain *"at the service of another type of progress, one which is healthier, more human, more social, more integral."*

As we navigate the evolving landscape of AI in the business world, the Pontiff's profound insight offers us a proven, reliable compass, regardless of whether or not you subscribe to his religion. AI's vast potential can be transformative and undeniably impactful to our planet and to us as a species, but we must ask ourselves this essential question: what kind of progress do we seek?

The answer can be found within each of us, in the heart of human-centered values and ethics. At its best, AI can revolutionize industries, create unprecedented efficiencies, and inspire previously unimaginable innovations. Yet, its true promise will only be realized when it is wielded with a deep respect for human dignity, community, and the common good.

Our exploration of artificial intelligence throughout this book has illuminated myriad ways that AI currently intertwines with businesses, workforce dynamics, creativity, and the broader societal fabric. Crucially, the future of this rapidly advancing technology must echo Pope Francis' divine wisdom about the indispensable role of our inherent human values, to ensure that AI serves not just economic growth, but human growth as well – a more inclusive, compassionate, and integral human progress.

Thanks to the increasing proliferation of technological wonders, our once far-off earthly future seems to come closer and closer with each passing day. Exciting though it is, at this speedy pace, we cannot lose sight of our necessary role as stewards of conscience. Leaders in every sector have both the privilege and the responsibility to shape this future, so that the dawn of the AI era produces not just smarter machines, but also ushers in a wiser, more empathetic world.

Pope Francis also once remarked, *"If mankind's so-called techno-logical progress were to become an enemy of the common good, this would lead to an unfortunate regression to a form of barbarism dictated by the law of the strongest."* His words should serve as a touchstone for any and all next-generation artificial intelligence technologies. Our collective mission, therefore, must be to safeguard human dignity – in every individual, community, and society – by certifying that technological progress, reinforced by AI, remains a steadfast ally of the common good.

Finally, it seems that AI is here to stay. But let's always remember that, while AI is a beneficial tool, it should never become more than that – a tool with which we construct a better future for humanity. People, guided by our compassionate hearts, creative minds, and precious souls, must always draft the blueprint. Here's to a future where technology helps us create the most rewarding human experience possible in our earthly lifetimes.

APPENDIX

Ten Guidelines for Ethically Integrating AI in Business

1. Put People Before Profits

- Ground each AI project in core values of human dignity, service, and the greater good, rather than mere efficiency or financial results.

- Ensure that applications address genuine societal needs and promote justice.

- Uphold the philosophy of "people over profits."

2. Be Examples of Transparency and Accountability

- Since opacity erodes confidence, promote trust by explaining AI decision-making in plain language whenever possible.

- Maintain clear responsibility for AI outcomes by understanding both the technological and ethical implications.

3. Safeguard Human Rights

- Protect privacy, autonomy and consent.

- Never compromise individual rights in the name of progress.

- Follow strict data regulations and inform users how data is applied.

- Emphasize that AI must always uplift humanity and never repress it.

4. **Foster Inclusivity and Equity**

- Proactively identify and counteract biases, because discrimination embedded in AI has the potential to scale exponentially.

- Uphold the dignity and worth of every person.

- Design AI to serve diverse communities justly.

5. **Advocate for Environmental Stewardship**

- Practice judicious stewardship by designing and utilizing AI systems that are sustainable and do not strain shared resources.

- Adopt forward-thinking development practices that preserve our planet for generations to come.

6. **Commit to Continuous Learning**

- Nurture a culture of lifelong learning and growth mindsets.

- Stay informed and updated on AI advancements and their ethical considerations.

- Foster continuous improvement, reflection, and adaptation, for no single solution is final.

7. **Cultivate Communities and Collaborations**

- Encourage diverse collaborations where various voices contribute to AI projects.

- Value insights from all stakeholders. Inclusive perspectives enhance outcomes.

8. **Maintain Integrity in Implementation**

- Rigorously test for biases and unintended harm prior to deployment, because flaws can scale exponentially.

- Post-launch, confirm that real world AI aligns with original ethical intentions, as progress without purpose will not endure.

9. **Implement AI as a Complement, Not a Replacement**

- Design and integrate AI technologies to augment human strengths rather than replace people.

- Remember that, at its best, AI can be an empowering partner.

- Continually evaluate if AI is enhancing work for your employees and all of society.

10. **Lead as Servants**

- Guide AI as wise stewards rather than passive implementers, while taking complete responsibility for its influence on users.

- Be compassionate leaders who create AI that promotes justice and empowerment for all people.